OFF TO KARNATAKA

SONIA MEHTA

PUFFIN BOOKS

An imprint of Penguin Random House

PUFFIN BOOKS

USA | Canada | UK | Ireland | Australia | New Zealand | India | South Africa | China

Puffin Books is part of the Penguin Random House group of companies whose addresses can be found at global.penguinrandomhouse.com

Published by Penguin Random House India Pvt. Ltd
4th Floor, Capital Tower 1, MG Road,
Gurugram 122 002, Haryana, India

First published in Puffin Books by Penguin Random House India 2017

Text, design and illustrations copyright © Quadrum Solutions Pvt. Ltd 2017
Series copyright © Penguin Random House India 2017

Picture Credits
P 7: Indian elephant (Alexander Mazurkevich/Shutterstock.com); P 9: Jog Falls, Karnataka (© Jughead i [GFDL (http://www.gnu.org/copyleft/fdl.html) or CC-BY-SA-3.0 (http://creativecommons.org/licenses/by-sa/3.0/)], via Wikimedia Commons); P 11: A peacock (© Jatin Sindhu (Own work) [CC BY-SA 4.0 (http://creativecommons.org/licenses/by-sa/4.0)], via Wikimedia Commons); P 13: Belgaum, Karnataka (© Mohsinkhadri (Own work) [CC BY-SA 4.0 (https://creativecommons.org/licenses/by-sa/4.0)], via Wikimedia Commons); P 14: Krishna Temple, Hampi (© Dey.sandip (Own work) [CC BY-SA 3.0 (https://creativecommons.org/licenses/by-sa/3.0)], via Wikimedia Commons), Mahishasura statue, Mysore (tantrik71/Shutterstock.com); P 16: Coins from the Kadamba dynasty (© Nijgoykar [CC BY-SA 3.0 (http://creativecommons.org/licenses/by-sa/3.0), via Wikimedia Commons), Emblem of the Gangas (© Jrsanthosh (Own work) [CC BY-SA 3.0 (https://creativecommons.org/licenses/by-sa/3.0)], via Wikimedia Commons; P 20: Quit India Movement (© Dore chakravarty [CC BY-SA 2.5 (http://creativecommons.org/licenses/by-sa/2.5), via Wikimedia Commons); P 24: Mysore Dussehra procession (Santhosh Varghese/Shutterstock.com); P 25: Dollu Kunitha (© Jackerhack [CC BY-SA 2.5 (http://creativecommons.org/licenses/by-sa/2.5)], via Wikimedia Commons); P 27: Nandi bull at Chamundi Hill, Mysore (AC Manley/Shutterstock.com); P 28: Wooden dolls (© Booradleyp (Own work) [CC BY-SA 3.0 (https://creativecommons.org/licenses/by-sa/3.0)], via Wikimedia Commons); P 29: Painting with gold leaves (© Dr. M. Muthukrishnan (Own work) [GFDL (http://www.gnu.org/copyleft/fdl.html) or CC BY-SA 3.0 (http://creativecommons.org/licenses/by-sa/3.0)], via Wikimedia Commons); P 30: A traditional house (Karthikeyan Gnanaprakasam/Shutterstock.com); P 34: Whispering gallery, Gol Gumbaz (© Santoshsmalagi (Own work) [CC BY-SA 3.0 (https://creativecommons.org/licenses/by-sa/3.0) or GFDL (http://www.gnu.org/copyleft/fdl.html)], via Wikimedia Commons); P 35: Bellary Fort (© Marc Roberts (originally posted to Flickr as Bellary Fort) [CC BY-SA 2.0 (https://creativecommons.org/licenses/by-sa/2.0)], via Wikimedia Commons); P 36: Hoyasaleshwar Temple (© Anks.manuja (Own work) [CC BY-SA 3.0 (https://creativecommons.org/licenses/by-sa/3.0)], via Wikimedia Commons); P 37: Dariya Daulat Bagh (suronin/Shutterstock.com); P 38: Bidar fort (© Tirumala Nalla (Own work) [CC BY-SA 4.0 (https://creativecommons.org/licenses/by-sa/4.0)], via Wikimedia Commons), Gagan Mahal (© Channveer.p (Own work) [CC BY-SA 4.0 (https://creativecommons.org/licenses/by-sa/4.0)], via Wikimedia Commons); P 39: Tarkash Mahal (© Santosh3397 (Own work) [CC0], via Wikimedia Commons), Fort garden (Santosh3397 (Own work) [CC0], via Wikimedia Commons); P 41: Tea plantation worker (Aleksandar Todorovic/Shutterstock.com); P 42: Mettur dam (© Vvenka1 [CC BY-SA 2.5 (http://creativecommons.org/licenses/by-sa/2.5)], via Wikimedia Commons); P 44: A road-side stall (Supamon R/Shutterstock.com), Patrode (© Radhikamprabhu82 (Own work) [CC BY-SA 4.0 (https://creativecommons.org/licenses/by-sa/4.0)], via Wikimedia Commons); P 54: Pillared corridor at the Chennakesava Temple, Mysore (© Claudine Van Massenhove/Shutterstock.com)

The views and opinions expressed in this book are the author's own and the facts are as reported by her, which have been verified to the extent possible, and the publishers are not in any way liable for the same.

The information in this book is based on research from bona fide sites and published books and is true to the best of the author's knowledge at the time of going to print. The author is not responsible for any further changes or developments occurring post the publication of this book. This series is not a comprehensive representation of the states of India but is intended to give children a flavour of the lifestyles and cultures of different states. All illustrations are artistic representations only.

ISBN 9780143440796

Design and layout by Quadrum Solutions Pvt. Ltd
Printed at Aarvee Promotions, India

www.penguin.co.in

Hello Kids!

I'm so happy you are reading this book. India is an incredible country and there are lots of things about it that we never get to hear about.

I discovered India because my father was in the Indian army. He was posted to many places all over India—and we dutifully followed him. Can you imagine that by the time I was in the tenth standard, I had changed nine schools? Of course it was hard making new friends almost every year, but the good part was that I got to live in so many places. Right from Kerala, where I was born, to Kashmir, Jhansi, Shillong, Chandigarh, Goa . . . the list is long.

Every time I go to a new place, I feel amazed at how different each state is from the other—and yet, how similar. Did you know that we can see monuments from the Stone Age right here in India? Or that we have more than twenty official languages, and most Indians know three or four on an average? Or even that some of the world's most amazing scientific marvels were invented in India?

Oh, there are many, many, many fun and fantastic things about the states of India, which we simply must get to know.

So get your backpack ready, get set to meet some new friends, and join me on a fun trip as we DISCOVER INDIA, STATE BY STATE.

I hope you enjoy reading this book as much as I have enjoyed writing it. I would love to hear from you. So do write to me at sonia.mehta@quadrumltd.com.

Lots of love,
Sonia Aunty

Mishki and Pushka have come to visit Earth from their home planet, Zoomba. They have never seen such an amazing place. Zoomba doesn't have trees and mountains and rivers like Earth does. But the people look exactly the same. When they come to Earth, they meet a sweet old man whom they call Daadu Dolma. Daadu Dolma shows them all the wonderful places in India and tells Mishki and Pushka all about them.

Mishki and Pushka can't believe what they see. They have seen a lot of Earth, but they have never, ever seen a place like India.

They are off to explore India state by state :)

Mishki

Mishki is a curious little girl. She is always asking loads of questions. On her home planet, she is always getting into trouble for poking her nose into things that are not her business.

Pushka

Pushka is Mishki's brother. He loves adventure. He is always ready for a new challenge. Whether it's climbing a mountain, or diving into a cold, cold sea, he is up for it.

Daadu Dolma

Daadu Dolma is a wise old man who has lived on Earth longer than the mountains and the seas. No one knows quite how old he is, but he certainly has been around. He knows everything about everything.

Mishki and Pushka are jumping up and down in excitement. They have a super fun adventure coming their way. They are going to explore the lovely state of Karnataka.

'What are we going to see, Daadu?' asks Mishki excitedly.

'Well,' replies Daadu, 'we are going to a state that is not only full of history but is also very modern. So you can expect to see lots of old monuments, meet some really great people and taste some of the best food you have ever tasted in your life.'

Mishki and Pushka clap their hands in delight. They pick up their backpacks and hold Daadu Dolma's hand. They are

OFF TO KARNATAKA!!!

Land ahoy!

Yes, Mishki. Karnataka has a lovely coastline and also has amazing forests. Come, let me tell you both a little about where this beautiful state is.

Look, Daadu. There are forests and the sea too in this state. They make it look so beautiful.

Knock Knock Knock

FRIENDLY NEIGHBOURHOOD

Karnataka has five states as its neighbours—and one vast sea as well. To its north are the states of Goa and Maharashtra. To its east is Telangana. To its south is Kerala and to its south-east is Tamil Nadu. And, of course, lapping its west is the Arabian Sea—which is why it has a long coastline.

ON THE MAP

To see exactly where **KARNATAKA** is on the map of India, go to

http://www.mapsofindia.com/maps/india/india-political-map.htm

FAB FOURSOME

Karnataka is divided into four main regions:
1. The coastal plains
2. The hills in the form of the Western Ghats
3. The Karnataka plateau
4. The black-soil tract

MAGICAL MALABAR

The long coast is a part of the famous and delightful Malabar region. This part is full of sand dunes and lagoons, making the soil rich and fantastic for farmers.

Psst! Malabar is also famous for its delicious food. Wait till we get to the food part to know more.

VOLCANIC ROCK

Regur

The black-soil tract actually has volcanic rock underneath the soil. This soil is called regur. It's great for growing cotton. But soil on the Karnataka plateau is not too fertile, except in the basins of the rivers.

FUN FACTS

State animal
Indian elephant

State flower
Lotus

State bird
Indian roller

State tree
Sandalwood

Western Ghats in Malnad

A FOUNT OF RIVERS

The Western Ghats make a sharp rise to reach a height of almost 3000 feet. This rising part is called Malnad. Some important rivers are born here that generously water the state, making it nice and fertile for farmers.

RUSHING RIVERS

Karnataka has some great rivers. The Sharavati, the Krishna, the Kaveri and the Tungabhadra are the main rivers. They rush down to the plains, watering the land along the way. Some go towards the plateau and some flow towards the sea.

SUMMER, WINTER, RAIN

Karnataka is not too hot, not too cold and not too wet. Through summer, the sun shines. Then come the rains. But winter hasn't begun yet. During the post-monsoon period, people bid the rains goodbye. And then comes a pleasantly cold winter, and out come the shawls.

JAUNTY JOG

The famous Jog Falls (also called the Gersoppa Falls) is on the Sharavati. This is one of India's highest plunge waterfalls. There are four smaller waterfalls on the way, with quaint names, like the Roarer, Raja, Rani and Rocket. And guess what, the force of this water is so strong that it generates lots of electricity for the state.

CRAZY CROSSWORD

Can you help Pushka solve this crossword puzzle with the help of these clues?

ACROSS

2. A smaller waterfall that makes the sound of a lion.
6. The Jog Falls generate a lot of this, helping light up homes.
8. The name of the long coast of Karnataka.

DOWN

1. This waterfall could take off into outer space.
3. Volcanic hard material.
4. Karnataka's beautiful state flower that Mishki loves.
5. This sea lies to the west of Karnataka.

WOODY WOOD

Wood is used to make different kinds of products.

There are many kinds of wood that the forests of Karnataka produce. The lovely fragrant sandalwood that is found here makes up a large part of the world's sandalwood. Imagine that! And that's not all! There are eucalyptus, teak, bamboo and rosewood trees too, all of which are used to make a lot of products, like dyes, varnishes and, of course, furniture.

CROP HOP

With so many rivers generously watering this lovely state, farmers have plenty to do. There are many crops that grow in abundance in Karnataka. Rice is grown all along the coast. Next in line are jowar and ragi. Lots of sugarcane is grown here too. Cashew, cardamom and betel nut are some of the other crops that farmers grow.

TREE TRIVIA

You'll find many trees in Karnataka. The Malabar Coast has lovely swaying coconut palms fringing the coast. The Western Ghats have a monsoon forest with a thick canopy of trees. And even the drier plains have scrub forests, which are forests with smaller trees and shrubs.

WILDLY WONDERFUL

The monsoon forests are home to elephants, tigers, wild cattle (also called gaurs), deer, wild boars, leopards and bears! The rains witness peacocks showing off their lovely plumes. There are many wildlife sanctuaries where these animals can roam freely, without being threatened by hunters.

The Bandipur Sanctuary is one of India's most famous sanctuaries. It has a large number of tigers, which are on the list of highly endangered animals.

TEA OR COFFEE, ANYONE?

There are many lovely tea and coffee plantations on the slopes of the Western Ghats. In fact, a lot of India's coffee comes from Karnataka.

JUMBLED WORDS

Can you unjumble these words so Pushka remembers what he has read so far?

ETA – _____ It grows in Karnataka but you drink it in a cup.

CRIE – _____ It's something people in Karnataka have with curry.

TUNOCOC – _____ These trees fringe the Karnataka coast.

KAET – _____ A strong wood from Karnataka forests that we can make furniture from.

CITY CITY BANG BANG

Karnataka has some of India's most beautiful cities. Some of them are super modern and some super ancient. But they are all beautiful.

BENGALURU (EARLIER BANGALORE)

This lovely city is also called the Garden City because it once had many, many beautiful gardens. Now it is called India's IT capital because there are so many super high-tech IT companies here. The whole world gets IT solutions from Bengaluru.

HUBLI

Hubli is called Chota Mumbai because it is supposed to be one of Karnataka's fastest growing cities. It is also called Hubali (which means flowing creeper) in Kannada, the language of the state. Hubli has a twin city called Dharwad, right next to it.

MYSURU (EARLIER MYSORE)

This city was the capital of the Mysore kingdom for over 500 years. It is rich in culture and has many lovely monuments.

VIJAYAPURA (EARLIER BIJAPUR)

With a rich history, this city has many historical monuments that tell us how advanced science was in India, even hundreds of years ago. (We'll know why later in the book.)

UDUPI

This city is a place of fantastic stories, amazing temples and beautiful beaches. But most of all, it is famous for its food and the Udupi cuisine. In fact, there are Udupi restaurants all over India.

BELAGAVI
(EARLIER BELGAUM)

Belagavi is an ancient city with a rich past. The locals like to call their city Kunda Nagari because you get a lovely sweet dish called kunda here. Belgaum is also called the sugar bowl of Karnataka.

13

Long, long ago

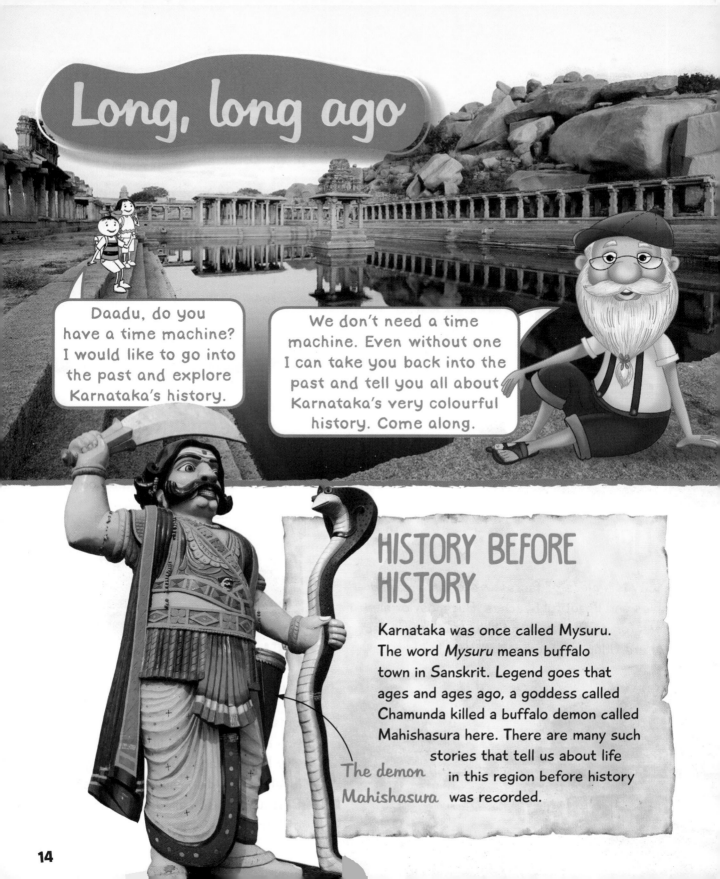

Daadu, do you have a time machine? I would like to go into the past and explore Karnataka's history.

We don't need a time machine. Even without one I can take you back into the past and tell you all about Karnataka's very colourful history. Come along.

The demon Mahishasura

HISTORY BEFORE HISTORY

Karnataka was once called Mysuru. The word *Mysuru* means buffalo town in Sanskrit. Legend goes that ages and ages ago, a goddess called Chamunda killed a buffalo demon called Mahishasura here. There are many such stories that tell us about life in this region before history was recorded.

MANY DYNASTIES

Karnataka, as we know today, didn't exist at one time. Karnataka, Tamil Nadu, Andhra Pradesh, Telangana—all of these were one region. There were many kings and dynasties that fought for control over this rich and fertile land. Just see how many dynasties ruled this land. Each of them built forts, palaces and temples during their rule.

1. Mauryas
2. Satavahanas
3. Kadambas
4. Western Gangas
5. Banas
6. Pallavas
7. Chalukyas
8. Rashtrakutas
9. Sangamas
10. Sevunas
11. Hoysalas
12. Wodeyars

SATAVAHANAS

The earliest rulers of this region were from north India, when the Maurya and Nanda Empires spread across India. Emperor Ashoka conquered the south but he was followed by the Satavahanas. They ruled for more than 300 years. During their rule, the languages Telugu and Kannada evolved.

FIND THE DYNASTIES

Many dynasties that ruled Karnataka are hidden in this word grid. Can you find them all?

M	A	U	R	Y	A	S	H	G	R	E	W	Q
Q	K	A	D	A	M	B	A	S	N	K	K	L
B	A	N	A	S	H	O	Y	S	A	L	A	S
W	E	R	T	W	O	D	E	Y	A	R	S	Q
S	S	E	V	U	N	A	S	Y	T	R	E	W
S	A	N	G	A	M	A	S	U	I	O	P	A
R	A	S	H	T	R	A	K	U	T	A	S	S
A	S	D	C	H	A	L	U	K	Y	A	S	D
P	A	L	L	A	V	A	S	L	K	J	H	F
M	N	B	V	X	Z	G	A	N	G	A	S	G

KADAMBA CONTROL

Gold coins

The Kadamba dynasty was one of the earliest dynasties. This dynasty was founded by King Mayurasharma. He and his successors set up many systems, minted gold coins and built many temples and palaces.

GANGA'S STYLE

Next came the Western Gangas, who were learned. They gave Karnataka its literary tradition. They also built beautiful monuments, like the famous Gomateshwar statue in Shravanabelagola (try pronouncing that big word).

Emblem of the Gangas

BADAMI BOOM

The Gangas became weak after many years of ruling. They were defeated by the strong Badami Chalukya dynasty. These kings loved their art and architecture. They were so strong that they even ruled other parts of India in Madhya Pradesh, Odisha and Gujarat.

MANY DYNASTIES COME AND GO

Many more dynasties ruled the region of Karnataka. Some, like the Rashtrakuta dynasty, spread to other parts of India. Each of them built monuments, palaces and temples in the styles they favoured. These monuments still exist today, like the Kailash temple in Maharashtra and the Mahadeva temple in Raichur. The Sevuna dynasty was known for their contribution to mathematics and music.

Bhaskaracharya was a great mathematician.

HAIL HAMPI

During this time, another great king made his presence felt in this region. Harihara I of the Sangama dynasty established the famous Vijaynagar Empire. He joined hands with other kings in the south to fight repeated Muslim invasions. This empire was known for its wealth and power. It was also during this period that music, arts and architecture reached amazing heights. The world-famous city of Hampi can still be visited and is an example of how advanced this civilization was.

Hampi has been declared a World Heritage Site by UNESCO, which means it is so precious that it must be conserved at any cost. This is because it gives us a rare glimpse into life thousands of years ago.

WHAT'S ODD?

In each of the rows below, there's one word that is odd. Help Mishki find it.

| CHALUKYAS | MAURYAS | WODEYARS | MING |

| CHENNAKESAVA | KAILASH | EIFFEL TOWER | MAHADEVA |

| SHRAVANABELAGOLA | ROME | VIJAYNAGAR | HAMPI |

INVADERS FROM THE NORTH

By this time, many kings from the Middle East and Persia had made inroads into several parts of north India. Their eye was now on the south. A sultan from Delhi, called Alauddin Khilji, finally defeated the ruling Hoysala king and with that, Islamic rule began in south India—and in the region of Karnataka.

THE SULTANATES OF KARNATAKA

Several sultans ruled this region for several hundred years. The Bahmani Sultanate was one of the first. A great Hindu king called Krishnadevaraya of the Vijaynagar Empire brought about the downfall of this dynasty. This was followed by the Bijapur Sultanate. A conqueror called Yusuf Adil Shah founded this empire. During his rule some wonderful monuments were built— including the Gol Gumbaz, which we will read more about later.

Krishnadevaraya of the Vijaynagar Empire

Muslim kings were called sultans.

HERE COME THE MUGHALS

The great Mughal Empire was spreading across India. It was left to Emperor Aurangzeb to overthrow the Bijapur Sultanate and take over the region. But not for long. The British were knocking hard on India's doors.

THE KINGDOM OF MYSORE

As the Vijaynagar Empire grew weak, the kingdom of Mysore grew strong. A family called the Wodeyars came to power. When they weakened, Hyder Ali, an able general, came to power. They lay low for many years. Much later, the British allowed them to rule under them.

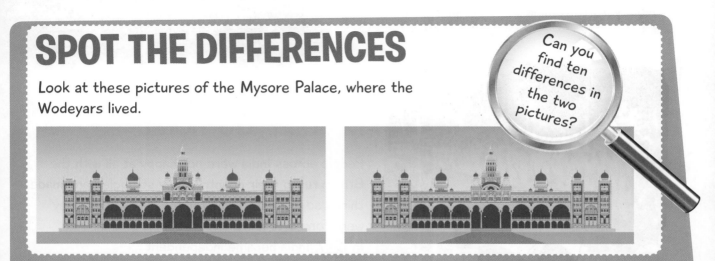

SPOT THE DIFFERENCES

Can you find ten differences in the two pictures?

Look at these pictures of the Mysore Palace, where the Wodeyars lived.

A MAJOR POWER

Hyder Ali was a strong king. He expanded his kingdom into other parts of India. His son Tipu Sultan was equally brave. Under them, the kingdom of Mysore became a major military power. But even they could not withstand the continuous attacks by the British. Finally, they were overthrown and Tipu Sultan was killed on the battlefield.

Tipu Sultan's army waged fierce battles with the British.

BRITISH AHOY!

The British soon took over the entire country. They snatched control of the Mysore kingdom too. They divided the state into separate provinces. They made the rules but allowed the Wodeyars to remain as rulers in name.

BRITISH, GO HOME!

People across India were not happy at all with the British ruling their country. They struggled and made things so uncomfortable for the British that they were forced to leave and free India of their rule. In 1947, India became independent.

LET'S SPEAK KANNADA

The Mysore Palace

The brand-new Indian government decided to reorganize India based on language. People in south India spoke Tamil, Telugu, Malayalam and Kannada. The Kannada-speaking population formed Mysore State. For many years, the maharaja of Mysore (still a part of the Wodeyar family) ruled it as governor general. Finally, in 1973, it was renamed Karnataka.

Whew!!! What a long history this state has!

TIPU'S MAZE

Mishki and Pushka want to help Tipu Sultan fight the British. But they are lost in this maze. Can you help them get out?

MANY, MANY DIALECTS

The language of Kannada has many dialects, which means there are different ways in which the language is spoken in different parts of the state. Many people living closer to the borders of Maharashtra speak a language called Konkani, which has some Kannada words in it too!

But now let's learn some proper Kannada words.

You.............Neenu
Come..........Baa
Here...........Illi
Me..............Naanu

Hello............Namaskara
More............Jaasthi
What?............Yenu?
How much/many?...........Eshtu?

Who?..............Yaaru?
Is it so?..........Houdha?

How?............Hege?
Where?...........Elli?
When?............Yavaga?
Why?...............Yake?

MATCH THE WORDS

Can you match the Kannada words to their English meanings? Pushka got mixed up.

Why?	Illi
Who?	Yavaga?
Here	Houda?
Is it so?	Yake?
When?	Yaaru?

A peep into their life

Oh! Look, Pushka, there is so much colour everywhere. Daadu, Karnataka seems like a colourful state.

That's for sure! As we saw, Karnataka has a rich history. Through thousands of years, different people have left behind styles of dance, music and festivals. That's what makes up culture. Let's experience Karnataka's lovely culture.

A MIX

There is a grand mix of people living here. Though the largest number are Hindus, there are many Christians and Muslims too! And there are many, many tribes who have different habits and cultures. And all this is reflected in the music and dance of the state.

SONG AND DANCE

Karnataka has many wonderful music and dance forms—both classical and folk. Let's see some of them.

DOLLU KUNITHA

This dance is performed by men and women to celebrate or remember an event. It could be a birth, a wedding—or even a funeral.

PUJA KUNITHA

This is a folk dance that is very colourful and a lot of fun. The dancers perform this when they worship Goddess Shakti. They use spectacular bamboo structures decorated with images of the goddess and perform amazing feats.

KAMSALE

This is a vigorous mix of dance and martial arts. Dancers enact the story of Lord Mahadeshwara Shiva. *Kamsale* is actually a bronze cymbal that they beat loudly.

UMMATTAATTU

Coorgi women wear a traditional red sari and dance in a circle to the beat of brass cymbals in devotion to Goddess Cauvery.

YAKSHAGANA

This popular song-and-dance form is great to perform and fun to watch. The theme is usually a story from the Ramayana or the Mahabharata. Groups of fifteen to twenty performers move from village to village. They start performing in the late afternoon and go on till dawn. Wow! That's long.

FANTASTIC FESTIVALS

Karnataka is full of exciting and colourful festivals. People celebrate all the national festivals like Diwali, Holi, Christmas and Eid with gusto. But there are also some other festivals that are celebrated in this region that we may not know about. Let's experience some of them.

RACING THE BUFFALOES

Kambala is a traditional buffalo racing festival that is spread over four months. Tracks are laid out in large paddy fields and buffaloes charge towards the finishing line. Large numbers of villagers cheer them on and the atmosphere is full of excitement and celebration. This custom began nearly a thousand years ago, when people prayed to god for a good harvest. Wow! Make sure you're not in the way.

THE EARTHEN POT FESTIVAL

Karaga is an ancient festival in which people pray to Goddess Shakti. On a full moon night, a grand procession is held, during which people pray and chant. They carry heavily decorated earthen pots and invoke the blessings of the goddess.

THE PEANUT FESTIVAL

In November, when the first groundnuts peep out of the soil, people celebrate this ancient festival. The story goes that every full moon night, a bull would charge across the field and ruin the groundnut crop. Farmers prayed to Basava Nandi (a bull god) to stop the bull. And that is how this festival was born.

A HARVEST FESTIVAL

Huthri is a festival of song and dance during which a good rice harvest is celebrated. For an entire week people celebrate and give thanks. Starting on a full moon night, farmers and their families perform a puja (prayer) and cut their crop only after this is done. Then, of course, it's time to celebrate—with great food, music and dancing too!

BULL RACE

This bull looks ready to race but is distracted by its shadow. Pushka wants to make sure nothing distracts the bull. Can you find its exact shadow so it can start the race?

A

B

C

OLD IS GOLD!

They say Kannada is one of India's oldest languages—after Sanskrit, Prakrit and Tamil. No wonder there is so much beautiful literature in Kannada. The people of this state are said to be well read and great lovers of the arts. Ancient poets, like Pampa and Ranna, have written beautiful poems in worship of god and about the Mahabharata.

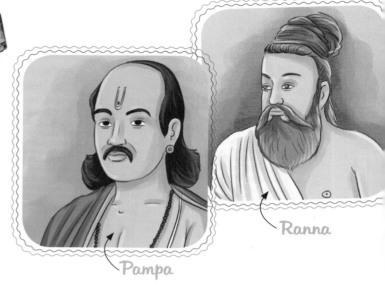

Pampa

Ranna

DOLLED UP

Doll making is another very big and popular craft. During the festival of Dussehra, doll makers exhibit their skills and marketplaces are full of colourful dolls—gods, goddesses, and people too! Even little children busily make tiny dolls for their parents and grandparents. Isn't that sweet?

CARVED IN STONE

Stone carving is centuries old. For generations, people have been carving beautiful sculptures. Did you know that sculptors identify stones as male or female? They craft gods from male stones and goddesses from female stones. They also have neutral stones that are used to carve birds and trees.

CARNATIC MUSIC

Carnatic music, which is popular all over south India, is very big in Karnataka. A musician called Shaarjnadava was one of the earliest performers of this style of music in Karnataka.

PAINTING PERFECTLY

The Wodeyars of Mysore were great lovers of painting and art. They encouraged craftsmen to develop this skill. Now, Mysore paintings, with gold leaf, are world famous for how detailed and beautiful they are.

Gold-leaf painting

TWIN DOLLS

Mishki has painted some dolls for Daadu Dolma. Can you find two dolls that are exactly alike?

A   B   C   D   E   F

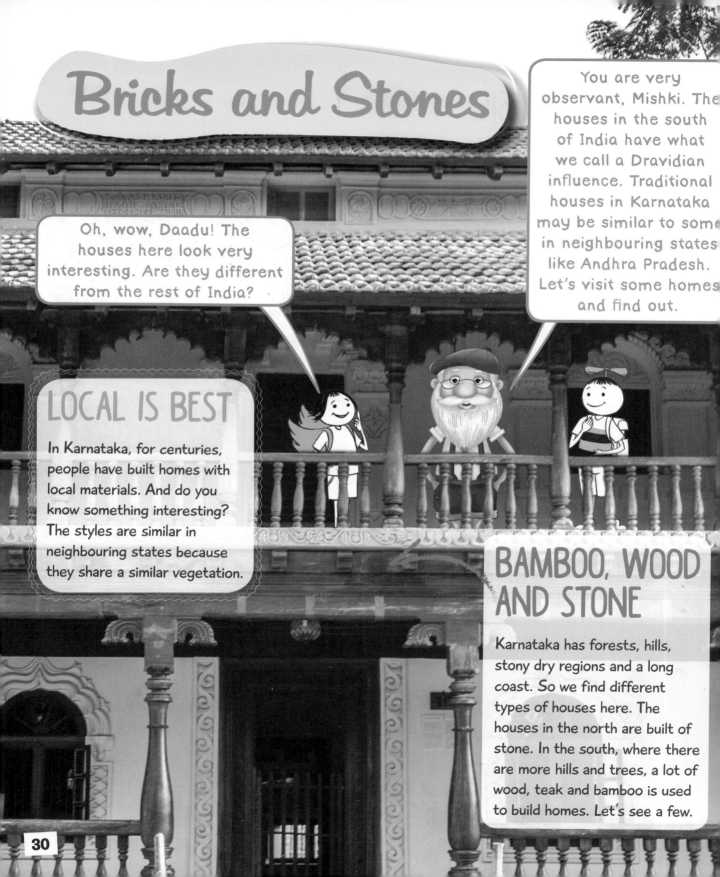

Bricks and Stones

Oh, wow, Daadu! The houses here look very interesting. Are they different from the rest of India?

You are very observant, Mishki. The houses in the south of India have what we call a Dravidian influence. Traditional houses in Karnataka may be similar to some in neighbouring states like Andhra Pradesh. Let's visit some homes and find out.

LOCAL IS BEST

In Karnataka, for centuries, people have built homes with local materials. And do you know something interesting? The styles are similar in neighbouring states because they share a similar vegetation.

BAMBOO, WOOD AND STONE

Karnataka has forests, hills, stony dry regions and a long coast. So we find different types of houses here. The houses in the north are built of stone. In the south, where there are more hills and trees, a lot of wood, teak and bamboo is used to build homes. Let's see a few.

GUTTHU HOUSES

These lovely houses were built hundreds of years ago by well-to-do families—especially by a community called the Bunts. The heart of this kind of a house was a large courtyard. Large joint families lived in these lovely homes, with the matriarch presiding over it all. The houses were cleverly built to catch the breeze and battle the heat of the region.

A matriarch is a woman who is the head of the household. When it is a man, he is called a patriarch.

KODAGU HOUSES

Near the region of Kodagu (which used to be called Coorg) lives a community called the Kodavas. At one time, very large joint families lived together in enormous ancestral homes called *ainemane*. The house had many rooms with many functions—like a granary where grains were stored, a temple room and so on.

SPOT THE HOUSE

There are so many types of houses in Karnataka. There are many other types in the world too. Draw a circle around the words that are types of houses that people live in.

MONASTERY   GARAGE   IGLOO   COTTAGE   MUSEUM

CHURCH   KODAGU   BARN   STABLE   HOSPITAL   BUNGALOW

MILL   EMBASSY   GUTTHU

Standing strong

Daadu, there have been so many kings who have lived here. There must be some amazing palaces and forts here.

You're right, Pushka. There are lots of amazing forts, palaces and temples. Come, we will visit some of the most interesting ones.

HAMPI

Let's start with one of the most marvellous sights in the world—the ruins of Hampi. Hampi was once the capital city of the golden empire of Vijaynagar. The Portuguese, the Arabs, the Persians and the East Asians all came here to trade. This incredible city is full of temples and carved pillars. Even the landscape is awesome, with giant boulders smiling down on the old city. Shut your eyes and try and imagine talented craftsmen and sculptors competing with each other to create such beauty.

A MUSICAL TEMPLE

The Vijaya Vittala Temple in Hampi has fifty-six musical pillars, which people say make the sound of fifty-six different musical instruments. When the evening sun shines on this lovely temple, it turns a glistening shade of gold.

The Mahanavmi Dibba (victory platform) is where kings must have celebrated their victories.

A massive stone chariot helps you imagine kings waving to their subjects.

MAGNIFICENT MASTERPIECES

Hampi is full of beautiful monuments, each one a masterpiece.

The gopura (tower) is where people believe Lord Shiva married Parvati.

Imagine this! Every year, people get together to celebrate the wedding anniversary of Lord Shiva and Parvati.

Elaborate steps lead to water tanks where the royals bathed.

The Lotus Mahal is a palace that has the shape of a lotus blooming in the golden sunlight.

The Hazara Rama Temple has wonderful stories of valour and gods carved in detail on its walls.

These are the mammoth stables where elephants were housed.

CHARIOT MAZE

Pushka is riding a chariot. Can you help him find his way to Daadu and Mishki?

A SCIENTIFIC MARVEL

In the bustling city of Vijayapura is a monument that defies science. The Gol Gumbaz is a structure that contains the tombs of Sultan Muhammed Adil Shah and his entire family. The entire monument is crowned by a massive dome that has the incredible whispering gallery. What is amazing about this is that even though the diameter of the dome is so vast, if you whisper very, very softly, that whisper can be heard right across the gallery, more than thirty-five metres away.

Say 'Hello' in the whispering gallery. What you will hear coming right back to you is 'HELLO HELLO HELLO HELLO HELLO HELLO HELLO HELLO HELLO' many times over. It's like magic, though it has a science behind it.

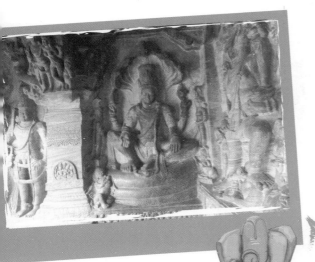

HARD ROCK

The city of Badami has amazing cave temples. These caves, which are thousands of years old, have a mix of Hindu, Jain and Buddhist carvings. These show gods and goddesses, scenes of war, horses charging and monks meditating. Imagine how hard sculptors must have worked to carve details on this rock!

THE KESAVA TEMPLE

In the city of Somnathpur, there is a star-shaped temple—the Kesava Temple. The walls have wonderful carvings of charging horsemen, mythological birds, beasts, horses and elephants, which show us the region's history. Sculptures of gods and goddesses and a breathtaking ceiling leave you gaping.

THE BELLARY FORT

This fort was built during the Vijaynagar rule. Legend says that the engineer who built it was hanged when the king saw there was a hill higher than the one the fort was built on, because he had wanted his fort to be on the highest hill. How cruel!

A GIANT STATUE

The statue of Lord Gomateshwara (or Bahubali) at Shravanabelagola is said to be the largest statue in the whole world made from a single stone. It was built by Chavundaraya— a minister from the Ganga dynasty.

The story goes that Bahubali stood without moving in deep meditation for one whole year. He stood so still that plants grew around his legs.

A GOLDEN TRIANGLE

Shravanabelagola Belur and Halebeedu are three cities people call Karnataka's Golden Triangle, because of their amazing monuments.

A TEMPLE MADE OF SOAPSTONE

The Chennakesava Temple in Belur has thousands of carvings made from black soapstone. This amazing temple was ordered to be built by a Hoysala king called Vishnuvardhana.

THE TEMPLE THAT SURVIVED

Halebeedu was once the capital of the Hoysala dynasty. The king ordered the Hoyasaleshwara Temple to be built. Sadly, the city was plundered and destroyed by invaders. This temple is one of the few things that survived.

TIPU SULTAN'S SUMMER PALACE

This beautiful palace is in Srirangapatna, near Mysuru. It is also called Dariya Daulat Bagh (which means from the wealth of the sea). It was built by the Muslim king Hyder Ali Khan and then finished by his famous son, Tipu Sultan.

A palace full of pillars and corridors

MYSURU PALACE

This palace was first built by the Wodeyars—the royal family of Mysuru. Lightning struck it and it was burnt down. The younger Wodeyars rebuilt it. Later, Tipu Sultan captured the palace, but it fell to ruin. After his death, back came the Wodeyars. During the wedding of a Wodeyar princess, it caught fire again and was burnt down. This time, when they rebuilt it, it lasted.

What resilience! The Wodeyars went to so much trouble, so we must see this wonderful palace.

Bidar is a beautiful and very historic little city that seems to take you right back into the past. It is full of amazing monuments that make history come alive. Let's go on a quick visit to Bidar.

THE BIDAR FORT

You might just feel like you are in *The Arabian Nights* when you enter this fort, because it is built in a Persian style by the sultans of the Bahmani dynasty. It has palaces, temples and tombs, all inside.

MAKE A GRAND ENTRY

You can enter the fort grandly through the Gumbaz Darwaza. This gateway has walls that are over twenty feet thick. That's as deep as an entire room! Right after, comes a smaller gateway called Sharza Darwaza.

THE THRONE PALACE

The Takht Mahal (*takht* means throne) was built by Sultan Ahmed Shah and was his main palace, though there are many other palaces in this fort.

THE HEAVENLY PALACE

Gagan Mahal is a magnificent palace that was built by a sultan. It has lots of courtyards, passages and wonderful rooms. They say the sultan built this for himself and his harem.

In those days, maidens used to entertain kings with song and dance. They were called the king's harem.

FIT FOR A TURKISH QUEEN

One of the sultans married a Turkish princess. He built a palace, that people call Tarkash Mahal, especially for her to live in. Perhaps he didn't want her to feel homesick, because this palace reminds you of buildings in Turkey.

HOW THEY LIVED

See how sultans lived! Imagine royal chefs cooking feasts in the palace kitchen. In the royal baths, imagine the queens with their handmaidens. A garden called Lal Bagh was where sultans and their queens strolled. There is even a cistern right in the middle of the garden.

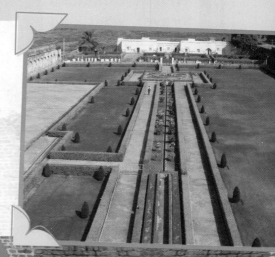

A cistern is a tank in which water is stored for daily use.

CRACK THE CODE

Pushka is pretending to be a spy during the Bahmani dynasty.
He is telling Mishki something in code. Help Mishki crack the code.

1 = X	2 = L	3 = P	4 = O	5 = T
6 = S	7 = E	8 = U	9 = R	

2 7 5   8 6   7 1 3 2 4 9 7

___ ___ ___   ___ ___   ___ ___ ___ ___ ___ ___ ___

Working hard

Daadu, if I lived in Karnataka forever, what kind of work would I have to do?

Oh, you will have many choices. There are big cities where people work in offices. There are tiny villages where people are farmers. And there are many other kinds of occupations too! Come, let us see what some of your options are.

FISHING AND FARMING

The largest number of people in this lovely state are farmers. They are busy growing rice, jowar and pulses. Karnataka also has lots of coconut, cashew and cardamom plantations. So cultivation of these also keeps farmers busy. There are also lots of fishermen here because of the long coast.

COFFEE OR TEA ANYONE?

There are many tea and coffee plantations, especially in Kodagu (or Coorg). Workers pick tea leaves and coffee berries, and work in the tea and coffee factories. Others work in companies that sell the final product. This area is carpeted with miles of tea plantations.

Collecting coffee beans

Picking tea leaves

A REAL GOLD MINE?

Oh wow! Real gold? Mines here have been producing gold since ancient times. The Kolar and Hutti gold mines have been around for centuries. The Kolar mines, once among the deepest in the world, are now shut. Miners go deep underground to look for gold.

Karnataka also has lots of diamond and iron ore mines, where lots of people work.

TECHIE LAND

Bengaluru has become a land of technology. There are many world-famous IT companies in Karnataka that supply IT services to the world. There are software and hardware engineers, coders and analysts—experts who make computers work.

Did you know?
When an IT professional from another country says, 'I am Bangalored', it means that their job has been given to someone in Bengaluru.

POWER PACKED

Thanks to Karnataka's gushing rivers, it has lots of hydroelectric plants that generate power and electricity not just for the state but also for other states as well. There are many engineers who work to achieve this.

Iron and steel mills

IRON FIST

As we saw, there is plenty of iron ore in Karnataka's soil. To make use of the iron and turn it into useful products, there are lots of iron and steel mills here, in which people work. It's a hot, tough job.

Silk being made

HERE WE GO ROUND THE MULBERRY BUSH

Both Bengaluru and Mysuru have many mulberry trees, where silkworms are reared. In fact, sericulture (the rearing of silkworms to create silk) has been an occupation since the time of Tipu Sultan. The mulberry silks made here are famous all around the world, and there are many weavers and agriculturists who work in silk farms.

Silkworm eating mulberry leaves

CROSSWORD TIME

Pushka and Mishki now know quite a bit about what people do for a living in Karnataka. Can you crack the clues and solve this crossword to see how much you remember?

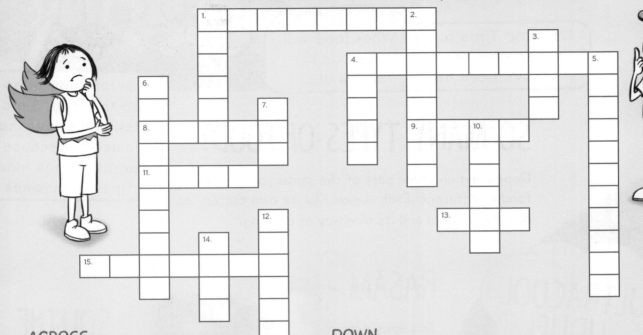

ACROSS

1. Farmers grow this spice in plantations. Hint: The opposite of DAD is hidden in this word.
4. These creatures live in mulberry bushes and give us a lovely material.
8. Something strong that goes with electricity.
9. We eat this with curry. A lot of this grows in Karnataka.
11. Another name for mud, in which we grow crops.
13. Farmers grow this but we drink it in a cup.
15. It sparkles and is very precious.

DOWN

1. This nut is also a fruit.
2. The bushes around which we go, and which breed silkworms.
3. A strong metal, and also an object with which we can make our clothes nice and neat.
4. Another strong material which we make in a mill.
5. A big word for breeding silkworms.
6. Hyder Ali's famous son.
7. Iron _____ (sounds like something used to row a boat, but spelt differently).
10. The brew our Mummy and Daddy love to have.
12. The new name for Coorg that is full of tea and coffee plantations.
14. It glitters and King Midas loved it.

Yum yum yum

Oh, yay! Time to eat! What food will we be able to enjoy here, Daadu? I have been hungry for a while.

SO MANY TYPES OF FOOD?

Depending on which part of the state you are in, the food is different. Each region has its own tastes, its own ingredients and its own way of cooking.

Before you jump into the food, I must tell you about the cuisine. Because Karnataka has many types of cuisines.

ULTRACOOL UDUPI

Udupi is like the kitchen of Karnataka. The food is strictly vegetarian, but no one can resist its call.

RASAM

This spicy pepper water is an important part of a meal. Careful! It can leave your eyes watering.

The food from Udupi is so famous that many restaurants that serve south Indian food are called Udupis.

SOUTHE GATTI

You must try these square dumplings, made of cucumber and steamed in banana leaves.

MASALA DOSA

This has a close cousin in Tamil Nadu and there is much debate about where it originated. People from Udupi believe it was innovated here. This pancake, stuffed with spicy potato, tastes really yummy.

MANGALORE MAGIC

There's some seriously yummy stuff from Mangalore. Here's a taste of some mouth-watering delicacies.

KORI-ROTTI

This incredible dish is made of wafer-thin bread served with spicy chicken curry

NEER DOSA

A divine pancake—white, soft and delicate.

SANNAS

These are fluffy-as-cotton idlis, made extra soft with a nice soak in toddy or yeast.

Toddy

PATRODE

This unique dish is made by steaming stuffed colocasia leaves.

KARNATAKA COOK FEST

There are many dishes that are popular across the state—no matter which region you are in. Ready to taste some of these?

CHITRANNA

This is a kind of a lemon rice with crunchy peanuts in it.

HALASINA HANNU MULKA

These are mouth-watering fritters made from jackfruit, which grows in plenty in this state.

MYSORE PAK

A flaky sweet dish, this is so full of ghee that you might feel a tad lazy if you eat a lot of it.

BISIBELEBHATH

This is a glorious mix of rice and dal, flavoured and spicy.

RAGI MUDDE

This dish is made of large balls of millet that are steamed and eaten along with mutton curry.

OOL KODAVA

Kodava cuisine is a hardcore meat-and-gravy kind of food. It is rather different from the rest of the food in Karnataka—just like its festivals and culture are different from those of the other parts of this state.

NOOL PUTTU

This dish is like stringy noodles, made in a special puttu maker. People have this with spicy curries or coconut chutneys.

VOTTI

Can you imagine a roti made of rice? That's exactly what a votti is. Sounds interesting!

PANDI CURRY

This is a spicy red meat curry that people love to eat with rice.

FOOD GRID

Can you find these yummy dishes in this food grid?

Votti
Rasam
Sannas
Patrode
Chitranna
Dosa
Ragi Mudde

R	A	S	A	M	D	S	A	S
F	V	O	T	T	I	U	Y	A
G	P	A	T	R	O	D	E	N
H	J	K	L	Q	W	E	T	N
C	H	I	T	R	A	N	N	A
P	P	W	I	Y	E	O	P	S
W	D	O	S	A	I	I	U	Y
Q	W	E	R	T	H	U	L	I
R	A	G	I	M	U	D	D	E

What to wear?

Look, what lovely colours, Daadu. I want to wear something like what those women are wearing.

They are wearing a typical sari, Mishki. Come, I will tell you about the clothes people wear in this state, and you can decide what you would like to wear.

VERY SARI

The traditional dress for women in Karnataka is a sari (they call it *seere*). But it's not worn in the same way that women wear it in the rest of India. Women drape it differently in different parts of the state.

Davani

Langa

THE HALF SARI

Langa davani is a 'half sari' that young girls wear. Langa means skirt and davani is a long cloth that is draped like a sari. Girls in other states of south India wear this too—but call it something else.

This is what I want to wear!

KODAGU STYLE

In the Kodagu region, the sari is worn very differently. See the picture? Can you tell the difference? Women even cover their head with a piece of cloth that matches with the

sari. This is called *vastra*. Though Coorg is now known as Kodagu, people still call this sari Coorgi style. The traditional clothing for men is a little different from the rest of Karnataka, as you can see in the picture above.

DRESSED TRADITIONALLY

Men wear either a lungi or a dhoti—both of which are long pieces of cloth, draped differently. A long cloth draped over the shoulder is called *panchey*. In some regions, men wear a turban called a *peta*. And a long traditional shirt called *angi*.

MODERN TIMES

As times have changed, more and more people wear modern clothes. But come festivals, people dress as traditionally as they can.

WEDDING WONDERS

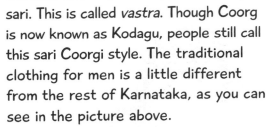

These lovely Kodagu couples are all dressed in their wedding finery. Can you spot ten differences in the two pictures?

Autograph, please?

Are all the famous people in Karnataka kings and queens?

Oh no, not at all! In fact, apart from its famous royalty, there are many people who have played an important part in the state. Some of them are not alive any more, but they are just as important. Let's meet some of them now.

GOPALA DASARU

He was a famous poet-saint who lived centuries ago. He wrote many kirtans (songs in praise of god) that are sung even today. He even had a pen name—Gopala Vittala.

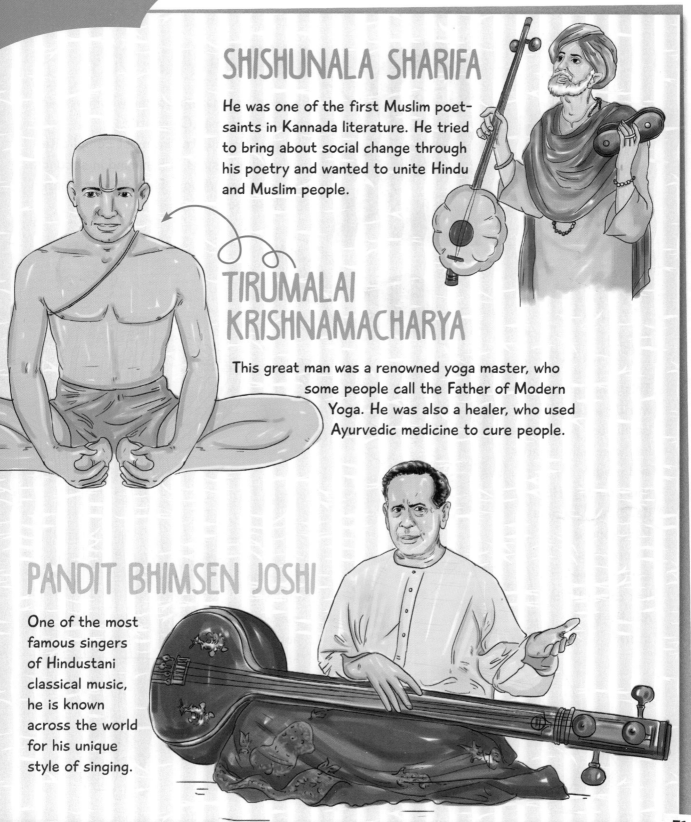

SHISHUNALA SHARIFA

He was one of the first Muslim poet-saints in Kannada literature. He tried to bring about social change through his poetry and wanted to unite Hindu and Muslim people.

TIRUMALAI KRISHNAMACHARYA

This great man was a renowned yoga master, who some people call the Father of Modern Yoga. He was also a healer, who used Ayurvedic medicine to cure people.

PANDIT BHIMSEN JOSHI

One of the most famous singers of Hindustani classical music, he is known across the world for his unique style of singing.

SHAKUNTALA DEVI

She was an amazing woman whom people called the Human Computer.
She could calculate the most complicated mathematical sums in her mind in seconds. They say even Albert Einstein was amazed at her ability.

PRAKASH PADUKONE

This athlete was a world-renowned badminton player, who has won many awards and medals for this country. His daughter Deepika Padukone is a gorgeous actress, who has taken Hindi movies by storm.

GIRISH KARNAD

He is an amazing playwright and actor, who has written, directed and acted in numerous plays and films—both in Kannada and Hindi.

RAHUL DRAVID

This incredible cricketer was born to Marathi parents in Indore, Madhya Pradesh. But he has lived in Bengaluru almost all his life. Dravid played for Karnataka initially and went on to play many matches for India. He was called The Wall because bowlers found it extremely difficult to bowl him out when he was in full form.

NANDAN NILEKANI

An unassuming but brilliant techie, he is a co-founder of the super successful company Infosys. He is also responsible for bringing to India its first unique identity programme, Aadhaar, by which every single Indian person has a unique identity number.

SUDOKU FUN

Mishki wants to be like Shakuntala Devi and be a whiz at math. Help her solve this number sudoku puzzle. Remember, all the numbers from 1 to 4 must be in each row and column, and each small square too!

1		4	3
	3		
2			
	4	2	1

Once upon a time . . .

Daadu, I would love to hear a story from Karnataka. I am sure there must be a lot of folktales.

Oh, yes, there certainly are. Karnataka has a rich tradition of folklore. Here's a story you will both like.

THE FOUR FOOLISH FRIENDS

Once upon a time, in a tiny village in Karnataka, there lived four foolish friends. They were good natured and friendly—but very, very foolish. Their names were Nanjayya, Chikkayya, Muthayya and Tukkayya. They did everything together. They ate together, worked together and spent all their free time together. You could say they were inseparable.

Their wives would get a little irritated by how much time they all spent with each other, but they had no choice.

Now it so happened that there was a big fair in the next town.

'Let us go to the fair and try our hand at making some money,' said Nanjayya.

'What a good idea!' agreed Chikkayya.

'But how shall we earn money?' asked Muthayya. 'We have nothing to sell.'

The four friends sat on a rock and thought hard.

'I know,' said Tukkayya suddenly, jumping up. 'Let us buy a nice buffalo and take it with us. We can then sell the milk and make lots of money.'

The others nodded excitedly. They thought it was a very fine idea indeed. So off they went to buy a buffalo.

The four friends went up to farmer Appaji who lived at the edge of the village.

'Appaji, we would like to buy your buffalo,' said Nanjayya.

'We will pay you well,' interrupted Chikkayya.

'Yes, and we will earn lots of money by selling its milk,' added Muthayya.

Appaji's eyes gleamed. Here was a chance to make some good money off these fools. His buffalo was in fine condition, but he charged much more than he would have otherwise, when he saw how eager the four were to buy it.

The four friends congratulated each other on their purchase. They had no clue that they had been overcharged. Off they went to the next town to the fair.

On the way, they had to cross a large river.

'How shall we cross this river?' said Nanjayya, scratching his head. 'I don't know how to swim.'

'Me neither,' said Chikkayya.

'Nor me,' added Muthayya.

'And I am scared of water,' whined Tukkayya.

'I know, let us all hold on to the buffalo. Buffaloes can swim. It will take us across safely,' said Nanjayya.

So the four friends held on tight while the buffalo took them safely across the river.

When they reached the other side, they looked at each other.

'Are we all here safe and sound?' said Nanjayya. 'I will count. One, two, three . . .'
He stopped. 'There are only three of us. One of us has drowned.'

'No, wait, I will count,' said Chikkayya. 'One, two, three . . .' He too stopped. 'You are right.
'There are only three of us. One of us has drowned.'

The other two started wailing.

'One of us has drowned. Oh! What shall we do?' they wailed loudly. The foolish men didn't
realize that each of them was counting the other three but not himself.

A trader was passing by. He saw the four foolish men sitting on a rock and weeping loudly.

'What's the matter?' he asked them.

'Four of us were on our way to the fair, but one of us has drowned,' Nanjayya explained
between loud sobs.

'I can see four of you,' the trader said, puzzled. 'See, one, two, three, four.'

The four friends stopped crying.

'You are right,' they cried, jumping up and down. 'None of us has drowned. You saved us!
Thank you so much.'

'What can we do in return for saving us?' asked Muthayya.

'Give me your buffalo,' the trader said slyly. He knew now how foolish the men were.

The four friends were so relieved to all be together that they happily gave away the buffalo,
and off they went back to their town, empty-handed, singing cheerfully all the way home.

TRAVEL DIARY

Have you enjoyed this trip to Karnataka with your friends Mishki and Pushka—and, of course, with Daadu Dolma?

Now you can make your own Karnataka diary. And if you ever visit Karnataka, make sure you take pictures and put them in the photo box.

The first place I would visit in Karnataka:

_____

If I ever meet Nandan Nilekani, this is what I would say to him:

_____

The one dish I am definitely going to eat:

_____

The monument I think is the most interesting:

_____

The one famous person from Karnataka I would love to meet:

_____

I think the most interesting historical figure from Karnataka was:

_____

The festival from Karnataka that I think is the most fun:

_____

The five words that I think describe Karnataka the best are:

_____

_____

_____

_____

_____

My Karnataka memories:

ANSWERS

page 31 SPOT THE HOUSE
KODAGU, GUTTHU, IGLOO, COTTAGE, BUNGALOW

page 33 CHARIOT MAZE

page 9 CRAZY CROSSWORD

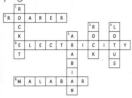

page 11 JUMBLED WORDS
TEA, RICE, COCONUT, TEAK

page 15 FIND THE DYNASTIES

page 17 WHAT'S ODD
MING, EIFFEL TOWER, ROME

page 19 SPOT THE DIFFERENCES

page 21 TIPU'S MAZE

page 23 MATCH THE WORDS
Why?—Yake?; Who?—Yaaru?; Here—Illi;
Is it so?—Houda?; When?—Yavaga?

page 27 BULL RACE
B

page 29 TWIN DOLLS
A and D are exactly alike.

page 39 CRACK THE CODE
LET US EXPLORE

page 43 CROSSWORD TIME

page 47 FOOD GRID

page 49 WEDDING WONDERS

page 53 SUDUKO FUN

1	2	4	3
4	3	1	2
2	1	3	4
3	4	2	1